BELMONT COUNTY LIBRARY

3 3667 00484 9060

J 294.5 QUI
Hinduism /
Quinlan, Julia J.,
33667004849060
MBE   05/2019

D1709412

HINDUISM

JULIA J. QUINLAN

Published in 2019 by Britannica Educational Publishing (a trademark of Encyclopædia Britannica, Inc.) in association with The Rosen Publishing Group, Inc.
29 East 21st Street, New York, NY 10010

Copyright © 2019 The Rosen Publishing Group, Inc. and Encyclopædia Britannica, Inc. Encyclopædia Britannica, Britannica, and the Thistle logo are registered trademarks of Encyclopædia Britannica, Inc. All rights reserved.

Distributed exclusively by Rosen Publishing.
To see additional Britannica Educational Publishing titles, go to rosenpublishing.com.

First Edition

Britannica Educational Publishing
J.E. Luebering: Executive Director, Core Editorial
Mary Rose McCudden: Editor, Britannica Student Encyclopedia

Rosen Publishing
Jacob R. Steinberg: Editor
Nicole Russo-Duca: Series Designer and Book Layout
Cindy Reiman: Photography Manager
Sherri Jackson: Photo Researcher

Library of Congress Cataloging-in-Publication Data

Names: Quinlan, Julia J., author.
Title: Hinduism / Julia J. Quinlan.
Description: First edition. | New York : Britannica Educational Publishing, in Association with Rosen Educational Services, 2019. | Series: Let's find out! religion | Includes bibliographical references and index. | Audience: Grades 1–5.
Identifiers: LCCN 2018017043 | ISBN 9781508106852 (library bound) | ISBN 9781508107163 (pbk.) | ISBN 9781508107279 (6 pack)
Subjects: LCSH: Hinduism—Juvenile literature. | Hinduism—Doctrines—Juvenile literature.
Classification: LCC BL1203 .Q56 2019 | DDC 294.5—dc23
LC record available at https://lccn.loc.gov/2018017043

Manufactured in the United States of America

Photo credits: Cover Kylie McLaughlin/Lonely Planet Images/Getty Images; p. 4 © Encyclopædia Britannica, Inc.; p. 5 Michael Benanav/Lonely Planet Images/Getty Images; pp. 7, 28 Frank Bienewald/LightRocket/Getty Images; p. 8 © Narayankumar/Fotoli; p. 9 Ullstein Bild/Getty Images; p. 10 Oleksiy Maksymenko/imageBROKER/Getty Images; p. 11 Evgenii Zotov/Moment Open/Getty Images; p. 12 NurPhoto/Getty Images; p. 13 Neale Cousland /Shutterstock.com; p. 14 © Photos.com/Thinkstock; p. 15 © Courtesy of the Victoria and Albert Museum, London/C. Cooper; p. 16 © Pramod Chandra; p. 17 © Photos.com/Jupiterimages; p. 18 Dawn L. Adam s/Shuttersstock.com; p. 19 Godong/Universal Images Group/Getty Images; p. 20 © TheFinalMiracle/Fotolia; p. 21 Dan Herrick/Lonely Planet Images/Getty Images; p. 22 Paul Fearn/Alamy Stock Photo; p. 23 AAron Ontiveroz /Denver Post/Getty Images; p. 24 Print Collector/Hulton Archive/Getty Images; p. 25 Dinodia Photos/Hulton Archive/Getty Images; p. 26 Raquel Maria Carbonell Pagola/LightRocket/Getty Images; p. 27 Travel Images/UIG /Getty Images; p. 29 Fizkes/Shutterstock.com; interior pages background Dmitry Chulov/Shutterstock.com.

CONTENTS

WHAT IS HINDUISM?

Hinduism is one of the world's oldest religions. Some Hindu traditions date back more than three thousand years. Over the centuries, however, its followers—called Hindus—have accepted many new ideas and combined

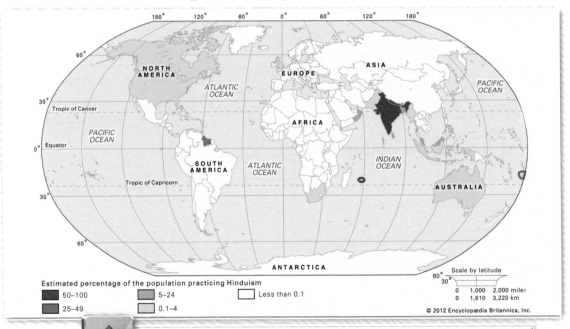

Estimated percentage of the population practicing Hinduism

- 50–100
- 25–49
- 5–24
- 0.1–4
- Less than 0.1

Scale by latitude

0   1,000   2,000 miles
0   1,610   3,220 km

© 2012 Encyclopædia Britannica, Inc.

This map shows the world distribution of Hindus. India has the world's largest population of Hindus.

A group of Hindus celebrate a festival along the Ganges River in India.

them with the old ones. More than nine hundred million people practice Hinduism worldwide. Most of them live in India, where Hinduism began.

Hinduism is different from other major religions because it has no founder. Its origins are lost in the distant past. It has several religious texts rather than one major text. No one has set down a list of beliefs for all Hindus to follow. Hinduism is diverse in belief and practice. Many sects and schools of philosophy coexist within Hinduism.

THINK ABOUT IT

Hinduism has no single founder. Can you think of the founders of other world religions? How does having a founder make religious worship different?

Beliefs and Sacred Texts

All Hindus revere the Veda, an ancient body of sacred writings. The word Veda means "knowledge." Hindus composed these texts in what is now India over hundreds of years, beginning in about 1500 BCE. For a long time, people passed down the texts of the Veda by reciting them. Eventually they wrote the texts down. Hindus today still study the Veda.

Hindus believe in a spiritual power called Brahman. Brahman is the source of all life and is present in every thing and every place. The human soul, called atman, is part of the universal Brahman.

> **Vocabulary**
> **Reciting** something means repeating it out loud from memory. This is how many ancient people passed down stories.

Hindus generally believe that when someone dies, the atman is reborn in another body.

A soul may return many times in human, animal, or even plant form. This idea is known as reincarnation. The idea of karma says that what a person does in the present life will

Devout Hindus read and study the ancient body of writings called the Veda, or "knowledge."

Nandi is a sacred bull figure in Hinduism. Devout Hindus practice nonviolence and do not eat meat.

affect the next life. The cycle of rebirth continues until one accepts that the atman (the individual soul) and Brahman (the universal soul) are one. Most Hindus consider breaking free from this cycle of rebirth to be a person's highest purpose.

Hindus are expected to follow the rule of ahimsa, which means "nonviolence" in Sanskrit, an ancient

THINK ABOUT IT

Cows represent wealth and abundance in Hinduism. Why do you think Hindus do not eat cows or other animals?

Maharishi Mahesh Yogi was a famous guru whose followers included the British rock band the Beatles.

language of India. This means that one must never wish to harm anyone or anything. Hindus consider many animals to be sacred. Devout Hindus do not eat meat.

A guru is a spiritual teacher or guide in Hinduism. The word guru means "venerable," or "honorable," in Sanskrit. Some gurus have founded their own sects, or schools, of Hinduism. In some sects, the guru is treated as the personification of a god on Earth.

PRACTICES

In Hinduism the act of worship is called puja. It can take different forms, from short daily rites in the home to long rituals in temples. In general, Hindus pray for a god to enter their home or a temple, and then treat the god as an honored guest. Temples vary from small village shrines to huge complexes—almost small cities—with walled courtyards, pools for ceremonial bathing, schools, hospitals, and monasteries. Religious services

VOCABULARY

Monasteries are places where religious people called monks live, work, study, and pray.

Hindus perform rituals and hold festivals in temples like this one in Toronto, Canada.

Hindus honor images of their gods with flowers, fruits, and other gifts.

are not held at particular times, as they are in many other religions.

The first act of temple worship is opening the temple door. Temple visitors may meditate or chant. Images or icons of the gods, called *murti* or *pratima*, are honored with gifts of flowers, fruit, or perfumes. Visiting worshippers are given small portions of holy food. When worshipping at home, Hindus also offer food or flowers to the gods and recite parts of the Veda.

Nepalese artists create a colorful mandala during a festival in Kathmandu, Nepal.

Tantrism is the search for spiritual knowledge and for release from the cycle of rebirth. It involves chanting sacred sounds and words called mantras and drawing symbols called mandalas.

Pilgrimages, or journeys to holy places, have been important in Hinduism since ancient times. Many pilgrimage sites lie in northern India along the Ganges River, which Hindus consider the holiest of rivers. They call it Mother Ganges. Hindus believe that bathing in its waters washes away sin. People have built many temples along the Ganges for cremating, or burning, the dead. They scatter the ashes on the river, believing that the dead will avoid the cycle of rebirth and go straight to heaven.

THINK ABOUT IT

Can you think of any holy places in other religions, like Islam or Christianity? Do people make pilgrimages to those places? Why or why not?

Hindus believe that the Ganges River is holy. They bathe in its water to purify themselves.

Main Gods

Hindus worship many gods. The worship of the gods Vishnu, Shiva, and Shakti make up the three major branches of modern Hinduism. Followers of Hinduism believe that the gods sometimes take on human or animal form. These forms of the gods are called avatars.

The god Vishnu is considered the protector and preserver of life. In Sanskrit his name means

Vishnu is one of the central gods of Hinduism. He is generally depicted as having blue skin and four arms and holding certain symbolic items in each hand.

COMPARE AND CONTRAST
Unlike Hindus, followers of Christianity and Judaism worship only one god. Can you think of some similarities between Hinduism and Judaism or Christianity?

"The Pervader." The worship of Vishnu and his avatars is called Vaishnavism. The most popular avatars of Vishnu are Krishna and Rama. Images of Vishnu often show him with his wife, Lakshmi.

The god Shiva represents the forces that create life as well as those that destroy it. The name Shiva is Sanskrit for "Auspicious One." Shiva takes different forms—such as a wandering beggar, a person who is half man and half female, or a dancer. The branch of Hinduism that is devoted to Shiva is called Shaivism.

The figure in the center of this painting is the Hindu god Shiva.

In this statue, Shakti is shown as Kali, a fierce giantess.

The supreme goddess is most often called Shakti. Like the god Shiva, Shakti can be either kind or fierce, depending on her form. As Parvati, she is a kind and beautiful woman. As Kali, she is a fierce giantess with black skin, a blood-red tongue, and large tusks. Kali carries an assortment of weapons and wears a necklace of human skulls. As mother goddess, Shakti stands for all aspects of nature, from birth to death. The worship of Shakti is called Shaktism.

Brahma is the creator god of Hinduism. He is generally depicted as having multiple faces and arms.

Brahma (not to be confused with Brahman) is considered the creator of the universe. In ancient times, he was widely worshipped, but his following is now small. Images of Brahma show him with four faces and four arms.

COMPARE AND CONTRAST

What similarities do you see between Vishnu, Shiva, and Shakti? What do they all have in common? What makes them different?

OTHER GODS

In addition to the three main deities, there are several other popular gods. Ganesa (or Ganesha) is the elephant-headed son of Shiva and Shakti. He is prayed to before

beginning a task or project. Lakshmi, the wife of Vishnu, is the goddess of wealth. Sarasvati is the goddess of learning and the arts. Hanuman is the monkey god associated with the adventures of Rama. In some areas of India, people worship Manasa, the goddess of snakes.

Many Hindu gods, like the elephant-headed god Ganesa, have features of both humans and animals.

 Hanuman is a monkey god. Monkeys are considered holy in Hinduism.

THINK ABOUT IT

Many religions guide or restrict what their followers can eat. Can you think of examples of food restrictions in other religions?

Many animals and plants are also regarded as sacred in Hinduism. Hindus believe the cow is especially sacred. All cattle are protected, and even Hindus who are not vegetarian do not eat beef. Monkeys and some snakes are also holy. Certain trees are considered sacred in Hinduism.

FESTIVALS

Hindu festivals take place throughout the year. They often last many days. Festivals include religious ceremonies, music, and dances. Diwali is probably the most popular Hindu holiday. It is a New Year celebration that lasts for five days in late October or early November. Diwali is celebrated by exchanging presents, eating festive meals, visiting friends, and lighting lamps and fireworks.

Another important festival is Holi. It is a spring festival. People throw colored water and powder on one another, and traditional roles are reversed. Sharad Navratri is a Hindu festival that takes place in early autumn,

Oil lamps burn during Diwali, the Hindu festival of lights.

During the celebration of Holi, Hindus throw colorful powder and water at each other.

usually over nine days. The festival celebrates the goddesses Durga, Lakshmi, and Sarasvati. It often ends with the Dussehra celebration on the 10th day. Dussehra marks the victory of Rama over the ten-headed demon king Ravana. People in southern India celebrate the harvest festival of Pongal in January.

COMPARE AND CONTRAST

Most cultures and religions have celebrations for the New Year. How is Diwali similar to other New Year celebrations? What makes it different?

HISTORY

In about 1500 BCE, a group of people invaded India from what is now Iran. They had a religion, called Vedism, that involved making animal sacrifices to the gods. They wrote the oldest parts of the Veda. Vedism was the starting point of Hinduism.

Over the years, the influence of other peoples and ideas made Hinduism a very different religion from Vedism. People began to disapprove of the killing of animals as sacrifices. The older gods of

VOCABULARY
Sacrifices are offerings to a god and can include killing an animal.

This illustration depicts the original Iranian invaders who brought Vedism to India in about 1500 BCE.

Sikhism grew out of Hinduism and Islam. These Sikh women pray during a religious ceremony in the United States.

Vedism were slowly replaced by newer ones. But some rites of Vedism have survived in modern Hinduism.

In the 1000s, Muslims invaded northern India. Islam, the religion of the Muslims, influenced some new schools of Hinduism. In the late 1400s, a new religion called Sikhism combined parts of Hinduism and Islam.

In the early 1800s, India became a colony of Great Britain. In response to foreign rule, Hinduism helped unify, or bring together, Indians against the British.

Geringer, Lith.

Lith. de Marlet & Cie du Rousin, N° 9.

Ram Mohun Roy was an important reformer who helped modernize Hinduism.

Also during this period, however, some Hindu leaders began speaking out against parts of traditional Hinduism. The reformer Ram Mohun Roy, for example, spoke out against the ancient form of social organization called the caste system. Under this system, people were treated differently depending on which social class they were born into. The reformers used some Western ideas to modernize Hinduism.

Mahatma Gandhi was an important Hindu political figure who made the idea of ahimsa, or nonviolence, popular.

THINK ABOUT IT

Just like the United States and Canada, India has many religions, including Hinduism, Buddhism, Sikhism, and Islam. Do you think having different religions has a good effect on a country's culture and people? Why or why not?

The most famous Hindu leader of the 1900s was Mahatma Gandhi. He brought the idea of ahimsa into politics. He helped win India's independence from Britain using only nonviolent methods.

MODERN HINDUISM

Most of the world's Hindus live in India. Today, India has a population of more than one billion people. More than three-fourths of the people living in India are Hindu. As the population of India

COMPARE AND CONTRAST

How might Hinduism change as it continues to spread to countries outside of India? How might it stay the same?

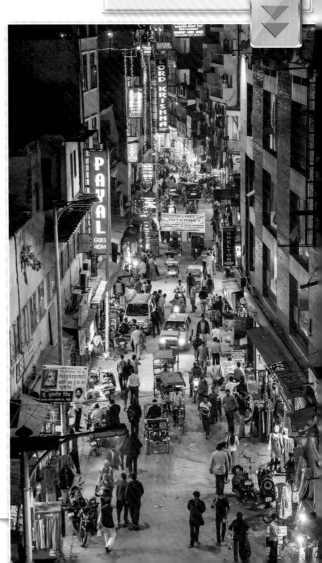

Shoppers crowd a bazaar in Delhi, India, at night. India has one of the world's largest populations.

Hinduism has spread to many countries, where beautiful temples such as this one in California serve local communities.

continues to grow, so too will the influence of Hinduism.

The migration of Hindus has spread the beliefs and practices of Hinduism around the world. Since the 19th century, large Hindu communities have formed in Africa, Malaysia, the islands of the Pacific Ocean and the Indian Ocean, and some islands of the West Indies. Since World War II, many Hindus have settled in the United Kingdom and in the United States.

A Hindu holy man practices traditional yoga alonside the Ganges River.

Hinduism's focus on nonviolence, karma, and meditation is very appealing to many people and has influenced many cultures around the world. Yoga and meditation are popular in the United States and in many other countries. Yoga is a system

VOCABULARY

Meditation is a mental exercise where a person sits quietly and focuses on their breath or a mantra. People do this to relax, to clear the mind, and to reach a higher level of awareness.

of training for the body and the mind. The word yoga means "union" in Sanskrit.

Hindus practice yoga to feel united with a higher power. They seek this union through posture (the position of the body), breathing, diet, and meditation. Today, many people who do not follow Hinduism practice yoga for exercise and relaxation.

Yoga is popular among many non-Hindus. Westerners practice yoga for its health benefits.

GLOSSARY

auspicious Showing or suggesting that future success is likely.

ceremonial Involved in a ceremony or religious event.

chant To speak with little or no change in tone.

coexist To live in peace with each other.

colony A territory under the control of a nation.

complex A collection of buildings.

devout Having a strong belief in a religion.

diverse Made up of many different parts.

mantra A sound, word, or phrase that is repeated by someone who is praying or meditating.

personification The representation of a thing or idea as a person.

pervade To be present throughout.

philosophy Basic beliefs about the way people should live.

reformers People who work to make something better.

revere To show devotion and honor to.

rites Important religious events or practices.

rituals Religious ceremonies.

sacred Holy; something important to a particular religion.

shrine A place of worship.

tusks Very long, large teeth that stick out when the mouth is closed.

universal Including everyone and everything.

vegetarian A person who refrains from eating meat and lives on a diet made up mostly of vegetables, fruits, grains, and nuts.

FOR MORE INFORMATION

Books

Aloian, Molly. *The Ganges: India's Sacred River*. New York, NY: Crabtree Publishing, 2010.

Amstutz, Lisa J. *Diwali* (Holidays Around the World). North Mankato, MN: Capstone Press, 2017.

Bartell, Jim. *India* (Blastoff! Readers: Exploring Countries). Minnetonka, MN: Bellwether Media, 2016.

Cohen Harper, Jennifer. *Little Flower Yoga for Kids*. Oakland, CA: New Harbinger Publications, 2013.

Lee, Michelle. *Holi* (World's Greatest Celebrations). New York, NY: Scobre Educational, 2016.

Meachen Rau, Dana. *Who Was Gandhi?* New York, NY: Penguin Workshop, 2014.

Websites

BBC
http://www.bbc.co.uk/schools/religion/hinduism

Kiddle
https://kids.kiddle.co/Hinduism

National Geographic
https://kids.nationalgeographic.com/explore/countries/india

INDEX